FOREWORD BY ROBERT FRICKE

GENUINE
CHRISTIANITY

STEVE KERN

For more information contact, Kern Enterprises, 2713 N. Sterling Ave., Oklahoma City. Ok. 73127 (405) 942-3504

All scripture references are from the New American Standard Bible, translated by the Lockman Foundation.

ISBN: 978-0-9798667-4-6

CONTENTS

FOREWORD

Do you want to know for sure you are a Christian and that you are going to heaven? Have you ever asked Christ to come into your heart? Did He come in? How do you know for sure He did? Do you want to grow in your relationship with Christ? Steve Kern's book will help answer these questions for you to realize these goals.

We are saved by grace through faith. God's part is grace; our part is faith. I believed Jesus came into my heart when I asked Him to because the Bible says so, and I know the Bible is true. Then I joined Campus Crusade for Christ staff to share the good news of the gospel with students on college campuses around the nation.

FOREWORD

Steve Kern and I are acquainted through a dynamic Christian fellowship group of about thirty amazing men who love God and love each other in the Lord. We meet weekly. One of us speaks to the group each week. Steve always blesses us with his insightful, inspiring words.

Steve has a love for God and for people, so he gives himself to minister to others. His desire is for people to come to know Christ and grow in an intimate relationship with Him.

Dr. Kern has written books based the beginnings explained in Genesis, about the sanctity of marriage, a commentary on the six days of creation with the science involved in it, and an explanation of reality to counter atheism.

May this writing bless you in your quest to know Jesus Christ.

-Robert Fricke

Author of *The Kingdom of God is Now,*
The Kingdom of God is Coming

INTRODUCTION

As a pastor I try to listen to questions my people are asking. One Sunday I had a young college student ask the question, "What is a Christian?" That question got my attention because it was asked by a church member who had been a Christian from childhood while growing up in a Christian home. Hearing the question I had to ask myself how many people in our church are asking the same question? Then it occurred to me that asking "What is a Christian?" could be another way of asking "How do I know I am a Christian?" or "How do I really know I am truly saved?" With all this in mind I began a study on what the Bible tells us genuine Christianity is supposed to look like. That study developed into a series of messages I preached to my church in the month of January, 2016. The major emphasis of those messages came mainly from I John 4 and 5.

In I John 5:13 the apostle John gives us his reason for writing this letter to the churches. This verse says, *"These things have I written to you who believe in the name of the Son of God , in order that you may know that you have eternal life."* John's reason for writing this letter was to answer the question, "What is a Christian?" or "How can I know for sure that I am saved?" This book will be following John's answer to these questions found in I John and other parts of the New Testament.

It is my hope that you will take what this book has to say to heart and use it to help you evaluate what your Christian experience has been so far to see if it measures up to what the Bible teaches us about being a genuine Christian. It may help you to realize your need to do what is needed for you to become a genuine Christian or help you to grow deeper in your relationship with Jesus Christ.

GENUINE CONVERSION TO CHRISTIANITY

"Whoever believes that Jesus is the Christ is born of God..." I John 5: 1, NASB

To begin my discussion of genuine Christianity I want to describe what it means to have a genuine conversion into the Christian faith. I will start with defining what I mean by **genuine** and **conversion**. Genuine is defined by the Webster's New World Dictionary as "authentic, ... being what it is said to be, ... real, true, authentic, not counterfeit or artificial." I am using the word **genuine** because it best communicates the point scripture makes that not all those who confess Jesus as Savior and Lord actually have a relationship with Him. Jesus Himself said *"Not everyone who says to Me, Lord, Lord, will enter the kingdom of heaven; but he who does the*

will of My Father." (NASB, Matthew 7: 21) Jesus also said that genuine Christians will be known not by their verbal confession only but by the things they do. That is what he meant by saying, *"... you will know them by their fruits."* (Matthew 7: 20) This book will describe what that **fruit** will look like in the life of a genuine Christian.

The word **conversion** is a New Testament word translated from the Greek word **epistrophe**. Vines Expository Dictionary of Biblical Words defines the meaning as "a turning from and a turning to." It implies the turning from the ways of the world and a turning to the ways of God. This turning is the result of a change of heart and mind brought about by the work of the Holy Spirit of God. Jesus describes this conversion in John 3 as being *"born again"* or being *"born of the Spirit."* The word **conversion** implies an obvious change or transformation that takes place in a person's way of life that expresses Christ- like qualities. A person's genuine experience of conversion begins with a conviction by the Holy Spirit of our separation from God that is a process developing saving faith.

Saving Faith

What is saving faith? R. C. Sproul, in his book *Defending Your Faith* (pp. 22-23), tells us that in the sixteenth century the church defined the three major elements of saving faith as notitia, **assensus**, and **fiducia**. These are the three major ingredients that bring about salvation in an individual's relationship with God. Hebrews 11: 6 says, *"And without faith it is impossible to please Him (God)."* (NASB) Yes, we must have faith but it must be a faith rooted and ground in what is acceptable to God.

Notitia, **assensus**, and **feducia** are three Latin words that actually describe a progression. The progression begins with **notitia** that refers to notes, data, or content of the gospel. What that means is saving faith begins with receiving the right information about Jesus Christ. Romans 10: 14 states, *"How then shall they call upon Him in Whom they have not believed? And how shall they believe in Him Whom they have not heard?"* (NASB) The Bible also says, *"So that faith comes from hearing, and hearing by the word of Christ."* (NASB, Romans 10: 17)

Some of the needed information that leads to saving faith is things like Jesus is God's promised Messiah in the Old Testament. In the New Testament He is referred to as the Christ which is the Greek word for the Hebrew word Messiah. It means anointed one. Not only is Jesus the Messiah, He is also the Son of God, born of a virgin Who lived a sinless life. We also need to know that He was sent by His Father to be crucified on a cross to pay the penalty for our sins through the shedding of His sinless blood. After being put to death, Jesus was buried in a tomb for three days before He arose again from the dead, and He did all this because He loves us. These are some of the fundamental things a person must know about Jesus Christ before they can have saving faith.

Once a person has been given this information, the next step in the saving faith progression is called **assensus**. It sounds much like the word assent and actually does mean intellectual or mental assent. At this stage after an individual has been given the necessary gospel information then that person must come to an agreement that what they have been told about Jesus Christ is true. Here is something important to know at this point. Mental assent in regards to the gospel is a step toward saving faith but it is not in and of its self saving faith.

James in his letter to the churches tells us that the demons believe the gospel but do not have saving faith.

The final step to saving faith is **fiducia**. This Latin word is taken from Roman law having to do with contracts meaning trust or confidence. When applied to the concept of saving faith, it describes a transition from mental assent to placing a personal trust and reliance in Jesus Christ out of a heart of love and gratitude for what Jesus has done for us. It is an embracing of Jesus Christ that begins a relationship that leads to a change of heart and mind. That completes the necessary components to arriving at saving faith.

The saving faith process is brought about by the work of the Holy Spirit. We will see now how this process is at work in a person's life who becomes genuinely converted after being genuinely convicted and then giving a genuine confession.

Genuine Conviction

Before genuine conversion can take place, the Holy Spirit must bring each person through becoming convicted of their sins. This conviction then develops a sense of need for Jesus Christ to forgive them of their sins. It is the Holy Spirit then Who gives each person the grace needed to be willing to confess that Jesus truly is the Son of God.

Jesus speaking of the Holy Spirit told us in John 16: 8, *"And He, when He comes, will convict the world concerning sin, and righteousness, and judgment."* (NASB) What did Jesus mean by using the word **convict**? The Greek word elencho means "...to convict, confute, refute, usually with the suggestion of putting the convicted person to shame." (Vines, ibid.., p. 128) Jesus is telling us that before a person can experience a genuine conversion we must come to realize that we are a sinner before God and that sin should cause us to feel guilt and shame.

I can remember this experience of conviction while sitting in church listening to the evangelist Freddie Gage preach about sin. I was a twelve year old boy who was taken to church every time the doors were open. I knew the Bible. I could answer all the questions my Sunday School teacher would ask. But I lived a secret life doing things with my friends that would have appalled my parents. While I sat there listening, all of a sudden I began to feel a deep guilt concerning all this stuff I was doing that I knew was wrong. This heartfelt conviction caused me to begin to pray to Jesus asking Him to forgive me. All of a sudden I felt a peace that caused me to know I was forgiven. I went forward that night and confessed Jesus as my Savior. I was baptized the next Sunday. That was the work of the Holy Spirit bringing me to a point of conviction.

As a pastor, when I am dealing with a child who wants to be saved, the first thing I do is to identify if that child has a concept of sin. Not only that he has a concept of sin but that he knows sincerely that he personally has sinned and knows he is a sinner. If that child shows a genuine admittance of their sin problem, that tells me the Holy Spirit has brought that child to the place of conviction in his life.

Not only should there be a conviction of sin, there should also be an awareness of an individual's lack of righteousness before God. That means that we understand in ourselves that we have no goodness in ourselves that we can offer to God to gain His acceptance. The other side of that coin is that if the gospel has been presented in such a way that lets an individual know that God accepts the righteousness of Jesus in our behalf when we put our faith and trust in Him, then we can find peace in His righteousness before God.

The Holy Spirit also convicts about the judgment to come. In the study of apologetics there is what is called the moral argument that is used as evidence for the existence of God. The argument is that because we as human beings all have a conscience there has to be a moral absolute Who established right and wrong. It is because of this conscience that we all have sense of guilt when we do something that is wrong and this sense of guilt brings with it a foreboding of a coming judgment that will right all that is wrong. The conviction of the Holy Spirit concerning a coming judgment is a confirmation of what we already know to be true within our God given moral conscience.

So then, as the Holy Spirit works in our hearts developing a saving faith, He is also bringing us to a genuine conviction concerning our sin, our lack of righteousness, and our date with a coming judgment before a holy God. When we surrender to that Holy Spirit's wooing of genuine conviction He has brought us to the point of speaking a genuine confession.

Genuine Confession

What is a genuine confession? The word **confession** Greek verb is homologeo which means "to speak the same thing." (Vines, p. 120) In the context of the process of **conversion** it is used to say the same thing the Holy Spirit says about Jesus Christ that He is the Son of God. As we fall under the conviction of the Holy Spirit concerning our sin, lack of righteousness, and the coming judgment the major objective is for us to come to the conviction that Jesus Christ, as God's Son, is God's only provision made available to us for doing away with our sin problem.

As we learn that the man Jesus was born of a virgin, lived a perfect sinless life, claimed to be the Son of God, prophesied His own death and resurrection, was crucified according to scripture, buried in a rich man's tomb for three days according to scripture, and then rose again according to scripture, and was witnessed by over 500 eye witnesses, that information is used by the Holy Spirit to cause us to agree with God's word and to openly proclaim that we believe that the man Jesus is the Christ, the Son of the living God. This is how the process of saving faith is developed in a person by the Holy Spirit that leads to a genuine confession that comes from a heart that truly believes Jesus is the Son of God.

The following verses speak of this genuine confession. *"...The word is near you, in your heart, that is the word of faith which we are preaching, that if you confess with your mouth that Jesus is Lord, and believe in your heart that God raised Him from the dead, you shall be saved; for with the heart man believes, resulting in righteousness, and with the mouth he confesses, resulting in salvation."* (Romans 10: 8-10, NASB)

John the apostle makes a similar statement, *"By this we know the Spirit of God: every spirit that confesses that Jesus Christ has come in the flesh is from God; and every spirit that does not confess Jesus is not from God..."* (John 4: 2-3, NASB) *"Whoever confesses that Jesus is the Son of God, God abides in Him, and he in God."* (I John 4: 15, NASB)

Jesus Himself said, *"Every one therefore who shall confess Me before men, I will also confess him before My Father who is in heaven. But whoever denies Me before men , I will also deny him before My Father who is in heaven."* (Matthew 10: 32-33, NASB) In other words, Jesus declared He is the Son of God by His birth, His message, His miracles, His death, His resurrection, and His ascension. When we are willing to agree with Him by declaring Him as the Son of God and receiving Him into our hearts as Savior and Lord we will experience conversion.

Genuine Conversion

Once a person experiences genuine conviction or what can be stated as becoming totally convinced of their sin problem and their need for God's saving grace through His Son Jesus Christ that causes them to genuinely confess Jesus as the Son of God out of a heartfelt convinced belief, that person experiences a genuine conversion. This **conversion** is a total work of the Holy Spirit of God.

Biblical conversion is the moving of the Holy Spirit from working alongside of a person to actually entering into the very essence of that person's being. Jesus described this conversion to His disciples when He said, *"And I will ask the Father, and He will give you another Helper, that He may be with you forever; that is the Spirit of truth, whom the world cannot receive, because it does not behold Him or know Him, but you know Him because He abides with you, **and will be in you.**"* (John 14: 16-17, NASB) **Conversion** is the Holy Spirit living in us.

Paul describes this conversion by referring to Christians as the temple of God in his first letter to the Corinthians, *"Do you not know that you are a temple of God, and*

19

that the Spirit of God dwells in you?" (I Corinthians 3: 16, NASB) He also described this conversion in II Corinthians 5: 17, *"Therefore if any man is in Christ, he is a new creature; old things passed away; behold new things have come."* (NASB) The new things that have come are the changes made possible in a person by the presence and work of the Holy Spirit.

The concept of genuine conversion leads us to ask the question, "What does this genuine conversion look like in practical terms?" This is a question we all need to ask ourselves as we are told in scripture to examine ourselves to make sure we know we are a true Christian. (II Corinthians 3:5) If we are a genuine Christian, what are we supposed to look like? This is important because Jesus said at the end of His Sermon on the Mount, *"Not everyone who says to Me, 'Lord, Lord,' will enter the kingdom of heaven; but he who does the will of my Father who is in heaven."* (Matthew 7: 21, NASB) Jesus tells us here that just because a person confesses Jesus as their Savior and Lord does not mean they have given a genuine confession. The confession is confirmed by a life that expresses a genuine conversion has taken place. In the next chapter we will look at what this genuine expression should look like.

GENUINE EXPRESSION
OF CHRISTIANITY

"So then, you will know them by their fruits."
Matthew 7: 20, NASB

The apostle John has given us the most direct description of the genuine expression of Christianity in his first letter to the churches in the fourth chapter. I John 4: 7-13, *"Beloved, let us love one another, for love is from God; and everyone who loves is born of God and knows God, for God is love. The one who does not love does not know God, for God is love. By this the love of God was manifested in us, that God has sent His only begotten Son into the world so that we might live through Him. In this is love, not that we loved God, but that He loved us and sent His Son to be the propitiation for our sins. Beloved, if God so loved us, we also ought to love one*

another. No one has beheld God at any time; if we love one another, God abides in us, and His love is perfected in us, because He has given us of His Spirit." (NASB) This passage makes it clear that the genuine expression of Christianity is having a love for God that causes us to love our fellow Christians and our fellow man.

Before I go any further it is important that I explain to you which kind of love John is referring to. The Greek language in the New Testament is often more versatile than English. The word **love** is a good example. In the Greek there at least three words that can be translated **love** in English. The three nouns are *erotikos, philanthropia,* and *agape.* The word erotikos is where the English word erotic was derived from. It refers to physical, sexual attraction. This kind of love is an emotional or physical sexual arousal when relating to the opposite sex. This Greek word is never used in the New Testament.

The second Greek word is *philanthropia* which combines *phileo (verb for love)* and *anthropos* the word for man meaning "love for man." (Vines, p. 382) The verb **phileo** is used in the New Testament when referring to human love or emotion that we have within family relationships, amongst friends, and close acquaintances.

The Greek city *Philadelphia* in Revelation 3 was known as "the city of brotherly love." This level of love is produced out of our fallen humanity. It is finite and limited by our selfish tendencies of self preservation.

That brings us to the third Greek word **agape**. In the New Testament *agape* is a higher level of love that rises far above **phileo**. Agape in its different forms is the word used in the I John 4 chapter. It refers to the kind of love that applies to God and the way that He loves. It is the love that the Holy Spirit produces in Christians who have been converted making it possible for a true believer to express God's love that goes beyond our limited ability to express *phileo* love.

Vines Expository Dictionary (p. 382) gives a worthy description of this kind of love: "**Love can only be known by the actions it prompts. God's love is seen in the gift of His Son, I John 4: 9-10. But obviously this is not the love of complacency, or affection, that is, it was not drawn out by any excellency in its objects, Romans 5:8. It was an exercise of the divine will in deliberate choice, made without assignable cause save that which lies in the nature of God Himself, Deuteronomy 7: 7-8.**

Love had its perfect expression among men in the Lord Jesus Christ...Christian love is the fruit of the Holy Spirit in the Christian, Galatians 5:22.

Christian love has God for its primary object, and expresses itself first of all in implicit obedience to His commandments, ... Self will, that is, self pleasing, is the negation of love to God.

Christian love, whether exercised toward the brethren or toward men generally, is not an impulse from feelings; it does not always run with the natural inclinations, nor does it spend itself only upon those for whom some affinity is discovered. Love seeks the welfare of all, ... and works no ill toward any, ... love seeks opportunity to do good to all men, and especially toward them that are of the household of faith, Galatians 6:10.

In respect to agapao as used of God, it expresses the deep and constant 'love' and interest of a perfect Being towards entirely unworthy objects, producing and fostering a reverential 'love' in them towards the Giver, and a practical 'love' towards those who are partakers of the same, and a desire to help others to seek the Giver."

I know the above quote is fairly long but I feel I could not have said it any better. To sum it up I can say that the agape love of God for us will cause us to agape love God and to agape love others. This agape love is a fruit only the Holy Spirit can produce in us. That is the **genuine expression of Christianity.** So let's see who this love for God and others was **promised** by God, **provided** by God, and is **performed** by God.

Promised by God

God knowing our fallen state understood our inability to keep His ultimate two commandments that sum up all His other commandments found in Moses' five books of the law gave us a **promise** that He would finally make it possible by giving us His Holy Spirit once again. I say once again because when Adam and Eve sinned against God in the Garden of Eden, God removed His presence from them in the person of the Holy Spirit who returns at genuine conversion.

If we could keep the two ultimate commandments of God, we could keep all of His commandments. What are those two commands? Jesus has told us in Matthew 22: 35-40, *"And one of them, a lawyer, asked Him a question, testing Him. 'Teacher, which is the great commandment in the Law?' And He said to him, 'You shall love (a form of agape) the Lord your God with all your heart, and with all your souls, and with all your mind'. This is the great and foremost commandment. And a second is like it, 'You shall love your neighbor as yourself.' On these two commandments depend the whole Law and the Prophets."* (NASB) Jesus quotes Deuteronomy 5:6 and then Leviticus 19:18 to show these summaries of the Law were already in the Law. History has shown as well as our personal experience that in our fallen state we are unable to keep these commandments perfectly so God has promised to make it possible by His Holy Spirit.

Where do we find the **promise**? The most clear statement of the **promise** is found in Ezekiel 36: 26-27, *"Moreover, I will give you a new heart and put a new spirit within you; and I will remove the heart of stone (hardened heart) from your flesh and give you a heart of flesh (softness). And I will put My Spirit within you and cause you to walk in my statutes (laws), and you will be careful to observe My ordinances (laws).* (NASB) Here God tells us that one day we will be able to keep His laws of agape love through a changed heart and the presence of the Holy Spirit living within us.

In Galatians 5: 22-23, the apostle Paul tells us how God makes this agape love possible in us. We have already seen where Jesus said the Holy Spirit would be within us. His abiding presence in us produces His fruit through us as we live in harmony with Him in us. That fruit is, *"... love (agape), joy, peace, patience, kindness, goodness, faithfulness, gentleness, self control."* (NASB) I believe Paul begins this list with love because the rest of the list are attributes produced by agape love. Paul goes on to write in verse 5:23-25, *" ...against such things there is no law. Now those who belong to Christ Jesus have crucified the (flesh through faith in Jesus) with its passions and desires. If we live by the Spirit, let us also walk by the Spirit."* (NASB) Notice Paul says *"against such things there is no law."* This is true because the agape love of God is the fulfillment of the law. It is living out the character of God Himself.

So the promise of God was to give us His presence in the person of the Holy Spirit. In doing so, God has made it possible for a Christian to keep His laws of love, not by our own fallen human power but by the power of the Holy Spirit. The next thing we need to see is how God **provided** for the coming of the Holy Spirit.

Provided by God

The **promise** to send the Holy Spirit was **provided by God** by sending His Son, Jesus Christ, to pay the penalty for all sin in order to make it possible for the Holy Spirit to come once again to live in the hearts and lives of true believers. The apostle John describes this provision in I John 4:9-10, *"By this the love of God was manifested in us, that God has sent His only begotten Son into the world so that we might live through Him. In this is love, not that we loved God, but that He loved us and sent His Son to be the propitiation (make us favorable to God again) for our sins."* (NASB)

Paul, in his letter to the Romans describes this provision for the coming of the Holy Spirit in Romans 8: 1-4, *"There is therefore now no condemnation for those who are in Christ Jesus. For the law of the Spirit of life in Christ Jesus has set you free from the law of sin and of death. For what the Law could not do, weak as it was through the flesh, God did: sending His own Son in the likeness of sinful flesh and as an offering for sin, He condemned sin in the flesh, in order that the requirement of the Law might be fulfilled in us, who do not walk according to the flesh, but according to the Spirit."* (NASB) Paul goes on to say, *"And if Christ is in you, though the body is dead because of sin, yet the spirit is alive because of righteousness. But if the Spirit of Him who raised Jesus from the dead dwells in you, He who raised Christ Jesus from the dead will also give life to your mortal bodies through His Spirit that dwells in you."* (Romans 8:10-11, NASB)

So the promise of the Holy Spirit to come and live in us was made possible by the sacrifice of Jesus Christ on the cross. Now that it is possible for the Holy Spirit to live in us we can learn to love God and our fellow man through Him, thus fulfilling the Law. Loving like this is the **genuine expression of Christianity**. But we must learn that this agape love can only be **performed by God**.

Performed by God

Paul wrote to the church in Thessalonica, *"Faithful is He who calleth you, who will also do it."* (I Thessalonians 5:24, KJV)The Lord gave us the command to love God and to love our neighbor. He never commands us to do anything that He does not plan to do by us through us. It is only by the Holy Spirit loving through us that we are capable of expressing agape love. Remember agape love is how God loves. Because our fallen nature is not capable of producing agape love, God has to do it through us. Jesus made this clear when He said, *"...for apart from Me you can do nothing."* (John 15: 5, NASB)

The genuine expression of genuine Christianity is having a love for God and our fellow man that comes from the presence of the Holy Spirit living in us. I John 4: 12-13 says, *"No one has beheld God at any time; if we love (agape) one another, God abides in us, and His love (agape) is perfected in us. By this (love for one another) we know that we abide in Him and He in us, because He has given us of His Spirit."* (NASB)

This agape love will manifest itself on different levels. It will express itself in our love for the Father, because he gave us His Son. I John 5:1 says *"Whoever believes that Jesus is the Christ is born of God; and whoever loves the Father loves the child born of Him."* (NASB) It will also produce a deep love for Jesus expressed by our obedience to Him. Jesus said, *"If you love Me, you will keep My commandments."* (John 14:15, NASB) We show our love for Jesus by the way we obey Him.

In loving the Father and the Son we will also love the brethren, our fellow believers. John wrote, *"Beloved, let us love one another, for love is from God; and everyone who loves is born of God and knows God."* (I John 4:7,

GENUINE EXPRESSION OF CHRISTIANITY

NASB) He also wrote in the same chapter, *"Beloved, if God so loved us (by giving His Son) we also ought to love one another."* (I John 4:11, NASB) If we have the love of God in us we will love who and what God loves.

God loves the lost of humanity as well. John 3:16 begins with, *"For God so loved the world..."* You can exchange the word **world** with the word **lost** and not change the meaning. Paul wrote God, *"...desires all men to be saved and come to the knowledge of the truth."* (I Timothy 2:4, NASB) Because God loves the lost, His Holy Spirit will cause us to love the lost as well. Paul expressed this love when he wrote to the church in Corinth, *"...I have become all things to all men, that I may by all means save some."* (I Corinthians 9:22, NASB) He refers here to saving the lost from going to Hell.

What is the True Expression of Christianity Then?

We all want know we have genuinely been converted. That is why John wrote the letter to the churches of his time. In I John 5:13 he gives us his reason, *"These things I have written to you who believe in the name of the Son of God, in order that you may know that you have eternal life."* (NASB)

How then can we know for certain that we have been genuinely converted? Is it because we walked down an aisle in some church or revival meeting and was then baptized? Is it because we had some kind of feeling when we said a prayer? Is it because we had some kind of ecstatic experience? Each of these different experiences may have been a part of your conversion but they are not the proof of your salvation.

No, Jesus said, *"A good tree cannot produce bad fruit, nor can a rotten tree produce good fruit. Every tree that does not bear good fruit is cut down and thrown into the fire. So then, you will know them by their fruits."* (Matthew 7:18-20, NASB) In other words our actions should match our profession.

So what is the kind of fruit Jesus is referring to? It is the fruit that only the Holy Spirit can produce through us. The fruit that is the outcome of God's love being expressed through us. It is that agape love that goes beyond ourselves and our fallen nature. It is that compulsion to do something when we see a need regardless of who the person is who has the need. And, it is that compulsion that comes from our love for God the Father and His Son our Lord and Savior Jesus Christ.

PETER'S LESSON

"Simon son of John, do you love Me more than these?" John 21: 15, NASB

The apostle Peter gives us an example of the difference that the Holy Spirit brings to a person's inability to express agape love. In the next chapter I will share with you the lesson we can learn from Peter's failure by his denial of Christ. He failed to stand with Jesus at His most challenging time of His ministry because he did not yet have the power of agape love to stand with Jesus.

The lesson begins in John 13:37-38 where we find Jesus and His twelve disciples in the upper room partaking of the Passover meal. During the meal Jesus tells the disciples that He was about to be betrayed by one of them and that He would be going away to a place where the disciples could not go with Him. In response Peter said to Jesus, *"Lord why can I not follow You right now? I will lay down my life for you."* (John 13:37, NASB) Once again Peter is the outspoken one giving a bold declaration of his loyalty to Jesus. But Jesus gave Peter a response he was not expecting when Jesus said to him, *"Will you lay down your life for Me? Truly, truly, I say to you, a cock shall not crow, until you deny Me three times."* (John 13:28, NASB)

Wow, what a slap in the face that must have been. That was as hard to deal with as when Jesus rebuked him with, *"Get behind me Satan!"* He had just told Peter He was going to build His church on the rock of Peter's confession that Jesus *"... is the Christ the Son of the living God."* (Matthew 16: 16, NASB) Jesus also told him that God had revealed this truth to Peter. So Jesus built him up and then took him down in the same conversation. It seems Jesus was determined to keep Peter humble. It was part of Jesus' preparation of Peter to make him ready to learn the most important lesson he would need to learn before God could use Peter to launch the Church as an instrument of the Holy Spirit.

Jesus brings the lesson home in John 21. By the time of this chapter Jesus has already appeared to the disciples after His resurrection two times. We learn in Matthew 28: 10 that Jesus told the disciples through the women at the tomb that He would meet the disciples in Galilee. While the disciples where waiting for Jesus, Peter and some of the other disciples decide to go fishing in the lake at Galilee. They fish all night and catch nothing. Early in the morning Jesus stood on the shore and called out to them to cast their nets on the other side of the boat. When they do so their nets filled with fish. That caused them to recognize that it was Jesus standing on the shore. Peter jumps in the water to swim to meet the Lord leaving the other disciples to drag the fish-filled nets to shore. When they came to where Jesus waited they found He already had a fire going and was ready to cook for their breakfast some of the fish they had just drug to shore.

After they finished eating, Jesus singled Peter out for some direct questioning. This discourse takes place in John 21:15-19 where Jesus begins with, *"Simon, son of John, do you love Me?"* Before I go any further let me remind you of the context of this conversation.

The time frame is only a week or so after the resurrection. Jesus met with the disciples the night of the resurrection on the first day of the week. It was a week later that He appeared again to the disciples to show Thomas, who missed the first meeting, His crucifixion wounds. This is now the third appearance of Jesus to the disciples. Not only was it a short time after the resurrection, it was all a short time after Peter had denied he knew Jesus three times before the cock crowed that crucifixion morning. I would like to speculate that the other disciples around the fire did not understand what was taking place between Jesus and Peter as Jesus questioned Peter's love. I believe this is true because I do not think the other disciples knew about Peter's denial at this time, but Jesus knew. It seems reasonable to assume that Jesus took this occasion to clear the air between Him and Peter.

Peter's Purpose

When Peter was first called by Jesus, he was a fisherman, the brother of Andrew, called Simon bar Jonas or son of John. But, when Jesus met him by the Sea of Galilee He told him, *"...you shall be called Cephas (which translated means Peter)"* (John 1: 42, NASB) Matthew 4: 18 tells us Jesus said to Peter and his brother Andrew,

"Follow me and I will make you fishers of men." (NASB) Peter must have been seen to be special by the other disciples because he was the only disciple who Jesus told his name would be changed. It seemed that from that early encounter Jesus had something special in mind for Peter.

Yes one day Simon son of John would truly be Peter the stone but he was going to have to go through a time of breaking and humiliation before that transition would take place. As time went on Peter did become the outspoken leader of the twelve and yet he also was the one Jesus rebuked the most. Of course his greatest failure would come when he boasted how he would die for Jesus and yet denied Him three times in a night before a cock crowed.

After that encounter Jesus reached out to Peter on the shores of the Sea of Galilee here in John 21 to let him know that Jesus remembered His call to follow Him three and a half years earlier. Even though Peter had failed miserably when it came time to stand firm in his commitment to Jesus, Jesus now lets Peter know He has not given up on the call He gave to Peter. This was a "God of the second chance" moment in Peter's life.

As we will see later Jesus refers to Peter as "Simon son of John" in this morning by the lake discourse. He had told Peter more than once that he was going to be called Peter, the stone, but at this point Jesus makes it clear that Peter has not yet become the stone he was to become. It is a reminder by Jesus to Peter of his fallen humanity as a son of another man, his father John. Peter has the need of learning that in his fallen humanity that he does not have the capacity to genuinely love Jesus in such a way that would embolden him to sacrifice his life for Jesus like he said he would do before his denial of Jesus.

So to summarize, Jesus wants Peter to know He still loves him. That he held no disappointment toward Peter. He also wanted to let Peter know He still planned to use him as His spokes person for His kingdom. He knew Peter would still become the stone taken from the rock of his confession that *"Jesus is the Christ the Son of the living God."* He also wanted Peter to know that he was not yet ready to sacrifice himself in behalf of Jesus until he received the Holy Spirit who was coming on the next Day of Pentecost. As we will see Jesus in John 21: 18 gives a hint that Peter would finally be able to give his life for Jesus in the future and allow him to redeem his word given to Jesus before his denial. What Jesus said was, *"...when you are old, you will stretch*

out your hands, and someone else will gird you, and
bring you where you do not wish to go."(NASB) He
was predicting to Peter concerning how he would be
crucified himself at the end of his life, which tradition
tells us took place. We are told Peter actually asked to
be crucified upside down because he was not worthy to
die like his Lord.

Peter's Phileo

This is a good place to explain the difference between
the two different Greek words used in this passage that
are translated **love**. The first Greek word is **phileo**. This
word is used to describe human love a person can have
for family members, and close friends. The city called
Philadelphia in Revelation 3 was referred to as the
city of brotherly love. This level of love was a human
emotion or connection that had its human limitations
due to our human, self preserving, fallen nature. **Phileo**
was the only level of love Peter had to offer Jesus. We
will soon see that it was not enough.

The second Greek word for **love** is **agape**. In the New
Testament this level of love was used in reference to
the kind of love that God expresses. Here is a summary
of the definition of this love I gave on page 11. This is

a love that goes beyond emotion. It is a love that loves regardless of worthiness or ability of reciprocation in the recipient of the love. It is a love that comes from the very being of who God is. John tells us that God loves because **God is love**. (1John 4:16) This is a love that reaches beyond our human capacity to love. It was the kind of love that caused Jesus to embrace the cross for Peter and all the rest of us.

Peter's Problem

Now let's go back to the conversation recorded in John 21: 15-19. It will show us that Peter had a twofold problem, pride and lack of power. Let's look into this conversation. *"So when they finished breakfast, Jesus said to Simon Peter, 'Simon son of John, do you love (agape) Me more than these?' He said to Him, 'Yes, Lord, You know that I love (phileo) You.' He said to him, 'Tend my Lambs.'"* (John 21: 15, NASB)

Notice Jesus called Peter *"Simon son of John"*, referring to his fallen humanity. He also makes the point that Peter had not become Peter the stone yet. Then He asked Peter if he loved Him *"more than these?"* Who or what are those *"these."* Some say it was the large catch of fish and Peter's love for fishing. I believe Jesus was referring to the other disciples and was asking Peter if he thought he loved Him more than the other disciples loved Him.

Jesus here exposes Peter's pride as being more committed to Him than his fellow disciples on the night of the Passover when Peter declared he was willing to die for Jesus suggesting the other disciples were not. Mark 14: 29 quotes Peter as declaring, *"Even though all (these other disciples) may fall away, yet I will not."* (NASB) By asking Peter, *"do you love me more than these?"* He is reminding Peter that he was just as cowardly as the rest of the disciples who fled and hid when Jesus was taken into custody. This question was meant by Jesus to humble Peter. But, but by saying, *"Tend My lambs,"* He leaves the door open to let Peter know Jesus still wanted him to be involved in His ministry; a statement of restoration of Peter back to acceptance in Jesus' call on his life.

Verse 16 goes on to say, *"He said to him again a second time, 'Simon son of John, do you love (agape) Me?' He said to Him, "Yes, Lord, you know that I love (phileo) You.' He said to him, 'Shepherd My sheep.'"* (NASB) In the first question above Jesus asked Peter if he had agape love for Him. He asks the same question again and Peter could only respond that he had phileo love for

Jesus. Even though Peter was not able to answer with agape love, he was at least honest. And again, Jesus lets Peter know He can still serve Him. The inference is that Jesus still agape loves Peter.

Now I come to the third question given in verse 17, *"He said to him a third time, 'Simon son of John, do you love (phileo) Me?" Peter was grieved because He said to him a third time, 'Do you love (phileo) Me?' And he said to Him, 'Lord, You know all things; You know that I love (phileo) You.' Jesus said to him, 'Tend My sheep.'"* Here Jesus truly humbles Peter by asking him if he even has the capacity to phileo love Him. This truly grieved Peter because the question exposed how even his human phileo love was restricted by his human, self serving, fallen nature. His lack of power was exposed. It is the same problem we all have in our inability to genuinely (phileo) love Jesus, let alone (agape) love Him in our own human power.

Peters Posterity

With the above discourse in mind, we learn Jesus' lesson to all of us through Peter is that we do not have the ability to (agape) love God or man without the Holy Spirit loving through us. So we see that Jesus was willing to reinstate Peter as His faithful follower because He knew Peter would finally be able to (agape) love Him when the Holy Spirit came.

As we saw earlier in verse 18, Jesus was able to predict Peter's future martyrdom because He knew the change that was going to take place in Peter as a person when the Holy Spirit filled him. Peter became a living example of the truth stated by Paul in Philippians 1: 6, *"For I am confident of this very thing, that He who began a good work in you will perfect it until the day of Christ Jesus."* (NASB)

The lesson Peter's experience teaches was stated by Jesus when He said, *"...for apart from Me you can do nothing."* (John 15: 5, NASB) and Paul said positively, *"I can do all things through Him (Christ) who strengthens me."* (Philippians 4: 13, NASB) In other words without Jesus we cannot even (phileo) love God or people without Him living in us by His Holy

Spirit. Paul agrees. He learned that Jesus living in him was what made it possible for him to sacrifice his life in behalf of the gospel of Jesus Christ. My point is that the Holy Spirit living in us and (agape) loving through us is the genuine expression of genuine Christianity. That is what we learn from Peter's lesson.

THE GENUINE PERFECTION
OF CHRISTIANITY

"There is no fear in love; but perfect love casts out fear..." I John 4: 18, NASB

What do I mean by the use of the word **perfection**. First let me tell you what I do not mean. When a person is genuinely converted, that does not mean that he is not going to sin anymore. The Bible does not teach sinless perfection except when referring to the person of Jesus Christ. We Christians will not be fully delivered from our sinful nature until we are transformed by the resurrection. We will not fully overcome sin until then, but we will begin to have victory over sin in such a way that sin no longer fully dominates our lives.

What I do mean is **genuine perfection** in the sense that John used the word **perfected** in I John 4: 17 where he writes, *"By this, love is perfected in us..."* *(NASB)* Here the Greek verb teleioo means "Bringing to completeness." (Vines, p. 466) It can also mean becoming mature. In other words the genuine perfection of genuine Christianity is growing into maturity or being made complete in our relationship with God through the working of the Holy Spirit in us. What does the Bible tell us that maturity or being complete looks like?

A Realization

Coming to **genuine perfection** is a process that begins with a **realization** of how much God actually loves us. I John 4: 9-10 tells us, *"By this the love of God was manifested in us, that God has sent His only begotten Son into the world so that we might live through Him. In this is love, not that we loved God, but that He loved us and sent His Son to be the propitiation for our sins."* (NASB) Each of the words translated into **love** are from the Greek word **agape** not **phileo**. The word **propitiation** means that Jesus, by shedding His blood to remove sin, made it possible for those who believe in Him to be restored to a positive love relationship with God.

This **realization** of how much God loves us is not something we come to on our own. It is the result of the work of the Holy Spirit illuminating our minds and then our hearts of the great price God was willing to pay to purchase our salvation. This illumination first breaks our hearts and then humbles us before God. This breaking and humbling leads to the beginning of the work of transformation in us from our old selfish fallen nature to our new self that is learning to love God more than self. (II Corinthians 5: 17)

You can know this transformation is taking place when you become more and more sensitive to sin in your life. I know that for myself personally that when I sin it grieves me to know that I have taken the love of God for me for granted. Paul expresses this kind of grieving in Romans 7: 24, *"Wretched man that I am! Who will set me free from this body of death?"* (NASB) The more we learn to realize the love of God for us the more our love for Him grows. It is just as John wrote in I John 4: 19, *"We love (God), because He first loved us."* (NASB)

A Reciprocation

To reciprocate means, "to return in kind or in the same degree." (Webster New World Dictionary) Coming to perfection or maturity begins to take place as we begin to agape not phileo God to the same degree that He has shown His love for us. That is what John meant when he wrote, *"We love (God), because He first loved us."* As we come to appreciate the great sacrifice God made for us through the death of His Son the response of **reciprocation** begins to grow. As the reality of *"For God so loved the world that He gave His only begotten Son..."* begins to dawn on us, genuine Christianity, that is produced by the Holy Spirit, will cause us to be willing to sacrifice ourselves in behalf of the Lord Jesus Christ.

We have already seen this transition take place in the life of Peter. Before Jesus went to the cross Peter said he was willing to die for Jesus; but when the time came to make good on his declaration he did not have the level of agape love in him to make it happen. But after witnessing the resurrection of Jesus and being filled with the Holy Spirit at Pentecost, Peter became a man ready to speak for Jesus, anywhere, anytime, even to the point that it cost him his life. Peter understood that

Jesus came to live and die for him and in Acts 2, Luke's witness concerning Peter after Pentecost we see that Peter was more than willing to live and die for Jesus. Reciprocation is always being willing to do for Jesus what He was willing to do for us.

Genuine perfection then takes place in a Christian when that person is ready to do anything that is put before them by God to do. I am reminded of the twenty-one Christian Egyptians dressed in orange prison jump suits and handcuffed who were marched in single file on the beach of Libya by ISIS Muslim extremists, made to kneel down and be beheaded, only because they were Christians unwilling to denounce their faith. The reports told us that they sang praises to Jesus as they shed their blood for Him. That's agape love.

We may not all be put in a position where we are required to die for our faith, but there are many ways we can deny ourselves and take up our cross and follow Him. Missionaries who leave family and nation to serve Christ in foreign countries are expressing agape love. Christians who give up their plans and dreams for carrier and personal gain to serve Jesus in ministry are expressing agape love. Christians who are willing to speak out for truth knowing it could jeopardize their job or grades in school or be labeled as some kind of religious fanatic are expressing agape love. This expressed agape love is our reciprocation to God for His agape love toward us.

A Re-integration

What I mean by a **re-integration** is a restoration back to a unified relationship with God. **Genuine perfection** is finally realized by a true believer in Jesus Christ when that Christian's relationship with God is no longer based on fear but based on love. John tells us, *"There is no fear in love; but perfect love casts out fear, because fear involves punishment, and the one who fears is not perfected in love."* (I John 4: 18, NASB)

What is John saying in this verse? As Christians we have not arrived at a level of maturity when our relationship with God is rooted and grounded in a legalistic mindset. So often our service to God is based on trying to **appease to please.** Our thinking is "if I don't do this then God won't do that." If I don't go to church then God won't do what I need Him to do for me next week. If I don't give my tithe to God then God won't give me what I want. If I don't pray and read my Bible everyday then God won't love me anymore. What I am describing here is a works relationship based on fear, not love. It is the idea that the things that I do for God are what make me acceptable to Him.

God does not want us to serve Him because we fear Him. He wants us to serve Him because we love Him. He wants us to attend church; He wants us to give our tithes and offerings; He wants us to pray and read our Bible everyday but He wants us to do these things because we know He loves us and that our love for Him causes us to do these things and much more because we love Him.

Let me ask you some questions. Do you attend church because you have to or because you want to? Do you give tithes and offerings because you have to or because you want to? Do you teach a Bible class or witness because you have to our because you want to? If you do these things because you have to then Jesus says, "forget it, I didn't go to the cross because I had to. I went because I wanted to. It was my love that compelled me. I want you to do no less for me." Acceptable service to the Lord is a service based on love.

Re-integration is described by John when he wrote in I John 4: 16, *"And we have come to know and have* *believed the love which God has for us. God is love, and the one who abides in love abides in God, and God abides in Him."* (NASB) This is the re-integration or the reestablishment of a person in a unified relationship with God based on God's love that has restored our agape love for Him that overcomes our phileo self love.

Romans 8: 1-4 describes this **genuine perfection** where Paul wrote, *"There is therefore now no condemnation (causing fear) for those who are in Christ Jesus (re-integrated). For the law of the Spirit of life in Christ Jesus has set you free from the law of sin and death (fear of judgment). For what the Law could not do, weak as it was through the flesh, God did; sending His own Son in the likeness of sinful flesh and as an offering for sin, He condemned sin in the flesh, in order that the requirement of the Law might be fulfilled in us, who do not walk according to the flesh, but according to the Spirit."* (NASB) I added the words in parentheses to show how these verses relate to my point that the love of God satisfying the death requirement of the Law's judgment of sin through Jesus Christ now allows us to relate to God on the basis of His love and grace not rules and regulations.

Notice what Paul said, *"He (Jesus) condemned sin in the flesh, in order that the requirement of the Law might be fulfilled in us, who do not walk according to the flesh, but according to the Spirit."* Walking according to the Spirit is walking in the love of God based on the understanding that we no longer have to fear the judgment of God because He has replaced His judgment with His grace made possible by Jesus Christ. It is the Holy Spirit that continually illuminates our minds and hearts to this reality of God's love.

What all this means is as we live our lives in God's love we no longer live with a fear of God's coming judgment but a hope and a joy of living in his presence in His coming kingdom. John sums it all up in I John 4: 17,*"By this, love is perfected with us, that we may have confidence in the day of judgment; because as He is, so also are we in this world."* (NASB) What does John mean by *"as He is"*? Jesus is loved by the Father. Jesus is accepted by the Father. Jesus is righteous before the Father. Because, we are in Jesus Christ by faith we are loved, accepted, and we are righteous before the Father in Him even while we live in this world.

Consider the following scenario. Suppose the world should ask you the following questions, what would your answers be? If your genuine Christian faith has been perfected by the Holy Spirit in Christ Jesus let me tell you what your answers should be:

Why do you go to church so much?
Because I love Jesus.

Why do you serve so much in church?
Because I love Jesus.

Why do you study the Bible so much?
Because I love Jesus?

Why do you fast and pray so much?
Because I love Jesus.

Why do you tithe and give so much to needs?
Because I love Jesus.

Why are you so faithful to your wife and kids?
Because I love Jesus.

Why do you help others so much?
Because I love Jesus.

Why are you such a good employee?
Because I love Jesus.

Why are you such a good student?
Because I love Jesus.

Why are you such a good neighbor?
Because I love Jesus.

Why are you so politically active?
Because I love Jesus.

Why do you love Jesus so much?
Because Jesus first loved me and gave Himself as a sacrifice to save me from my sin. How can I do anything less for Him? So whatever Jesus loves that is what I love.

That is the genuine perfection of the genuine Christian.

CONCLUSION

The original question that was asked of me that became the inspiration for this book was "What is a Christian?" It was asked by a young person who had grown up in church; made a profession of faith; was baptized and had been taught the Bible by devout Christian parents. I got the impression that what this person was really asking was, "How can I know that I am a Christian?" or "How can I know I am really saved and going to heaven?"

We all deal with the concept of security of the believer at some point in our lives. I hope my explanations of what a genuine conversion, genuine expression, and genuine perfection have given you my reader some answers of at least some things to think about as you compare your life experience to what I have shared.

I considered sharing some real life testimonies of people who I believe are living examples of being genuine Christians. As I thought about it the thought occurred to me that not everyone's experience is the same. It is also true that each person is living at different levels of growing as a genuine Christian. I was afraid some of you might be wrongly convinced that you are not a Christian because your experience has not reached a level of those persons whose stories I would tell.

I think the better approach is for me to encourage you to think through what I have shared with you in this book and then ask the Holy Spirit to show you what He wants you to know. If you truly are a born again Christian the Holy spirit will give you peace about it. He also will show you where you can learn to express your love for the Lord and others more effectively. If you have not yet experienced a genuine conversion, the Holy Spirit will convict you about your need to surrender fully to the Lord Jesus making a public confession that you

CONCLUSION

are convinced that He is the Christ, the Son of the living God. The following is His promise to all those who believe:

"Everyone therefore who shall confess Me before men, I will also confess him before My Father who is in heaven." (Matthew 10: 32, NASB)

What Kind of Love

What kind of love would give His crown in exchange for a cross?
What kind of love would count the gain worth much more than the loss?

What kind of love would pay the price for those who wouldn't care?
What kind of love is that to you, a joy or a snare?

What kind of love would take our sins and bare them all alone?
What kind of love would take us in and make us feel at home?

What kind of love would pay the price for those who wouldn't care?
What kind of love is that to you, a joy or a snare?

What kind of love would leave His place before His Father's throne?
What kind of love would become flesh sinners to atone?

What kind of love would do an act that say I really care?
What kind of love is that to you a joy or a snare?

What kind of love would take our sins and bare them all alone?
What kind of love would take us in and make us feel at home?

What kind of love is that to you, a joy (pause) or do you care?

SOURCES

Geisler, Norman L., Turek, Frank, 2004, *I Don't Have Enough Faith to Be an Atheist*, Crossway Books, Wheaton, Illinois.

Kern, Steve, 2001, *Judgments Greatest Question*, Kern Enterprises, Oklahoma City, Oklahoma.

Kern, Steve, 2007, *No Other Gods*, Kern Enterprises, Oklahoma City, Oklahoma.

Lyle, Jason, 2009, *The Ultimate Proof of Creation*, Master Books, Green Forest, Arkansas.

McDowell, Josh, McDowell, Sean, 2009., *Tyndale House*, Carol Stream, Illinois.

Morris, Henry M., 1976, *The Genesis Record*, Baker Book House, Grand Rapids, Michigan.

Morris, Henry M., 1989, *The Long War Against God*, Baker Book House, Grand Rapids, Michigan.

Sproul, R. C., 2003, *Defending Your Faith*, Crossway, Wheaton, Illinois.

JUDGMENTS GREATEST QUESTION

Dr. Kern's testimony and philosophy of ministry
as the pastor of an inner city church in Oklahoma
City, Oklahoma. **The book is based on the fast
God has chosen in Isaiah.**

EDEN'S VEIL

This is the first book in a three part trilogy.
It is an adventure novel written in the context
of the preflood environment based on a literal
creation interpretation. It is the story of a man
seeking truth in a fallen evil world. He is a
descendent of Cain in search of the Garden of
Eden. The introduction gives an overview of the
preflood. **It gives an alternative to evolution
explanations of how the world began.**

EDEN'S SON

This is the second book in the three part trilogy. After finding the garden through a great deal of hardship the hero of the book fins peace and meaning. **This book tells the story of his adventures and hardships he faces as he returns to tell his people about the one true God.**

EDEN'S TEARS

This is the third book in the three part trilogy. It tells the story of the hero in his later years and what the world was like leading up to the flood. The story transitions to Noah and his family as they build the ark and finally spend the year on the ark. **The book captures many of the possible difficulties Noah and his family faced during that time.**

NO OTHER GODS

Dr. Kern's signature book on creation. It is a verse by verse commentary on the first 11 chapters in Genesis. **It covers the creation, the fall,the flood, and the tower of Babel using science, archeology, and other apologetic arguments to show a literal, historical interpretation is the proper interpretation.**

GOD'S ANSWER TO THE QUESTION OF EVIL

The existence of evil is one of the major
arguments used by anti God detractors to justify
their atheism. **This book gives a clear explanation
why belief in God and the existence of evil
is the more reasonable understanding
of reality.**

THE SIX DAYS OF CREATION

A day to day commentary on the six days
of creation week and the seventh day of rest.
Dr. Kern wrote this in partnership with
Dr. Norbert Smith, an accomplished author
and professor of zoology. **This is an insightful
study given from a theologian and a scientist
who accept the literal creation interpretation
of Genesis.**

GOD'S PURPOSES FOR MARRIAGE

Marriage is the first institution that was
established by God in the sixth day of creation.
The Genesis account gives four major purposes
that God intended for marriage to fulfill.
**This book describes those purposes and why
it is important for men and women who enter
into a Bible based marriage relationship to make
these purposes guiding principles for
their marriage.**

www.ingramcontent.com/pod-product-compliance
Lightning Source LLC
Chambersburg PA
CBHW060704030426
42337CB00017B/2752